NOT ME!

Written by
Deb Mortensen

Illustrated by
Carissa Harris

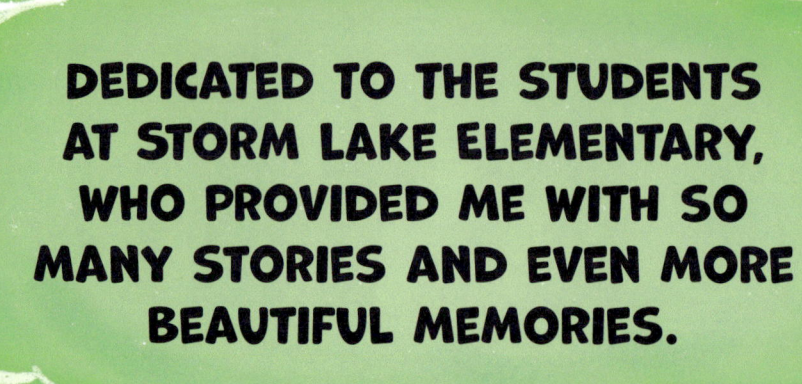

DEDICATED TO THE STUDENTS AT STORM LAKE ELEMENTARY, WHO PROVIDED ME WITH SO MANY STORIES AND EVEN MORE BEAUTIFUL MEMORIES.

Copyright ©2024 Deb Mortensen

Written by Deb Mortensen
Illustrated by Carissa Harris

Photograph of Deb Mortensen by Life Touch
Photograph of Carissa Harris (self-photo)

Published by Miriam Laundry Publishing Company
miriamlaundry.com

All rights reserved. This book or any portion thereof may not be reproduced or used in any manner whatsoever without the express written permission from the author except for the use of brief quotations in a book review.

HC ISBN 978-1-77944-186-7
PB ISBN 978-1-77944-185-0
e-Book ISBN 978-1-77944-184-3

FIRST EDITION

About the Author

Deb Mortensen is a retired elementary educator in Storm Lake, Iowa, where she taught for 39 years. Her love of writing began as a child when she would carry books, her Big Chief tablet, and crayons wherever she went. Mrs. Mortensen has written hundreds of poems, skits, music programs and loves to journal daily. She was awarded "Iowa's Reading Teacher of the Year" and has spoken on various literacy topics throughout the Midwest. Mrs. Mortensen enjoys reading, traveling, music, and being with children. Her debut children's book, *Not Me*, was inspired by the many students she had the priviledge of teaching.

Deb can be contacted via social media at Deb Mortensen Books.

 @Deb Mortensen Books

 @debmortensenbooks

About the Illustrator

Carissa Harris is an Australian artist who started drawing from an early age, taking inspiration from picture books, comics, and her favorite animated films. She studied Graphic Design and Animation before becoming an illustrator. Now she spends her days drawing with a hot cup of coffee and a good podcast or audiobook on in the background. Although she works digitally, her artwork emulates the traditional illustration styles of the classic children's books she loved as a child.

Joshua Bentley woke up early and put on his lucky shirt and new shoes. It was the first day of school. "This year is going to be super-duper!" Joshua exclaimed to his twin sisters at breakfast.

POOF!

On his way to school, Joshua felt something strange on his shoulder. As he tried to brush it away, he heard whispering in his ear.

Hi, Joshua! My name is Not Me.

"What?" Joshua exclaimed, turning his head and rubbing his eyes. "Am I imagining things?"

Susie didn't notice the creature on Joshua's shoulder. "I am so glad we are in the same class," she said. "My brother said Mrs. Kind is an awesome teacher!"

Joshua wasn't listening.
He was too busy scowling at Not Me.

When the bell rang, the two friends walked to Room 101 and sat on the rug. Mrs. Kind said, "Children, each day we will begin with a morning meeting and share our feelings."

Susie said, "I'm excited to see my friends again."

Christian said, "I'm nervous about going to a new school."

Joshua didn't say anything.
He was too worried about Not Me.
Am I the only one who can see him?
He thought.

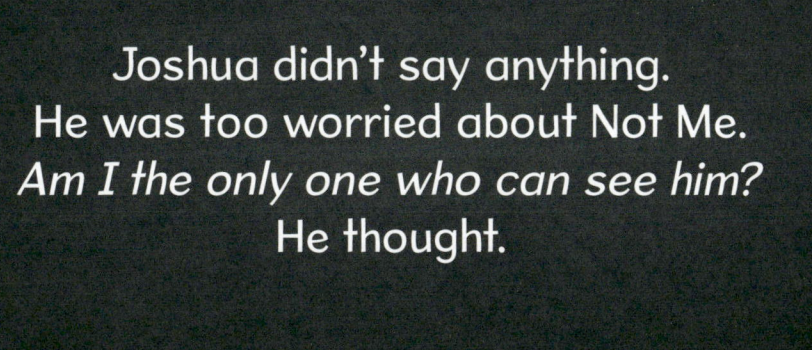

Soon, it was time for gym. "Welcome, everyone!" Mr. Fast said. "Today we're going to learn how to throw a frisbee." Joshua beamed. He had played frisbee with his dad all summer long.

He and Susie began tossing the frisbee back and forth.

Mr. Fast was hit in the head with a frisbee!

"Who threw that?" Mr. Fast demanded.

Mr. Fast turned around to see Joshua's bright red face. "Joshua," Mr. Fast warned. "Be more careful, little buddy."

"But—" Joshua began. Mr. Fast blew his whistle and gym class was over.

Back in the classroom, Mrs. Kind introduced Hermie the Hamster. "Hermie is our class pet," she explained. All the children gathered around the cage and ooh-ed and ah-ed.

I don't like those beady eyes and sharp teeth!

Soon, it was reading time. Everyone chose a book from the book basket. On his way back to his spot, Joshua opened the cage to give Hermie a scratch.

The children jumped up and began hunting for Hermie. By lunchtime, Hermie still hadn't been found. Everyone was very worried.

In the lunchroom, Señora Fork announced, "Today we are having pizza and peas."

Joshua did NOT like peas. He frowned when Señora Fork gave him an extra-large serving. Joshua whispered to Christian, "She can GIVE me peas, but I don't have to EAT them."

Christian whispered back. "I dare you to shoot some of your peas across the cafeteria."

Joshua laughed. He wanted the new kid to like him. He picked up his straw and…

Señora Fork yelled, "Who hit me with their peas?"

The kids around Joshua giggled.

After lunch, and out in the playground, Joshua joined a game of soccer. He kicked the ball really hard.

Back in Room 101, Mrs. Kind said, "I still haven't found Hermie. Everyone, please be careful as you move around." The children were counting various objects at their tables. When math ended, Mrs. Kind asked who would stay in from recess and help look for Hermie.

Everyone turned to stare at Joshua. He clapped his hand over his mouth. "I ... I mean..."

Joshua knew he was in trouble. His friends were disappointed. Mrs. Kind escorted Joshua to the principal's office. Joshua was afraid his family would be just as disappointed when they found out.

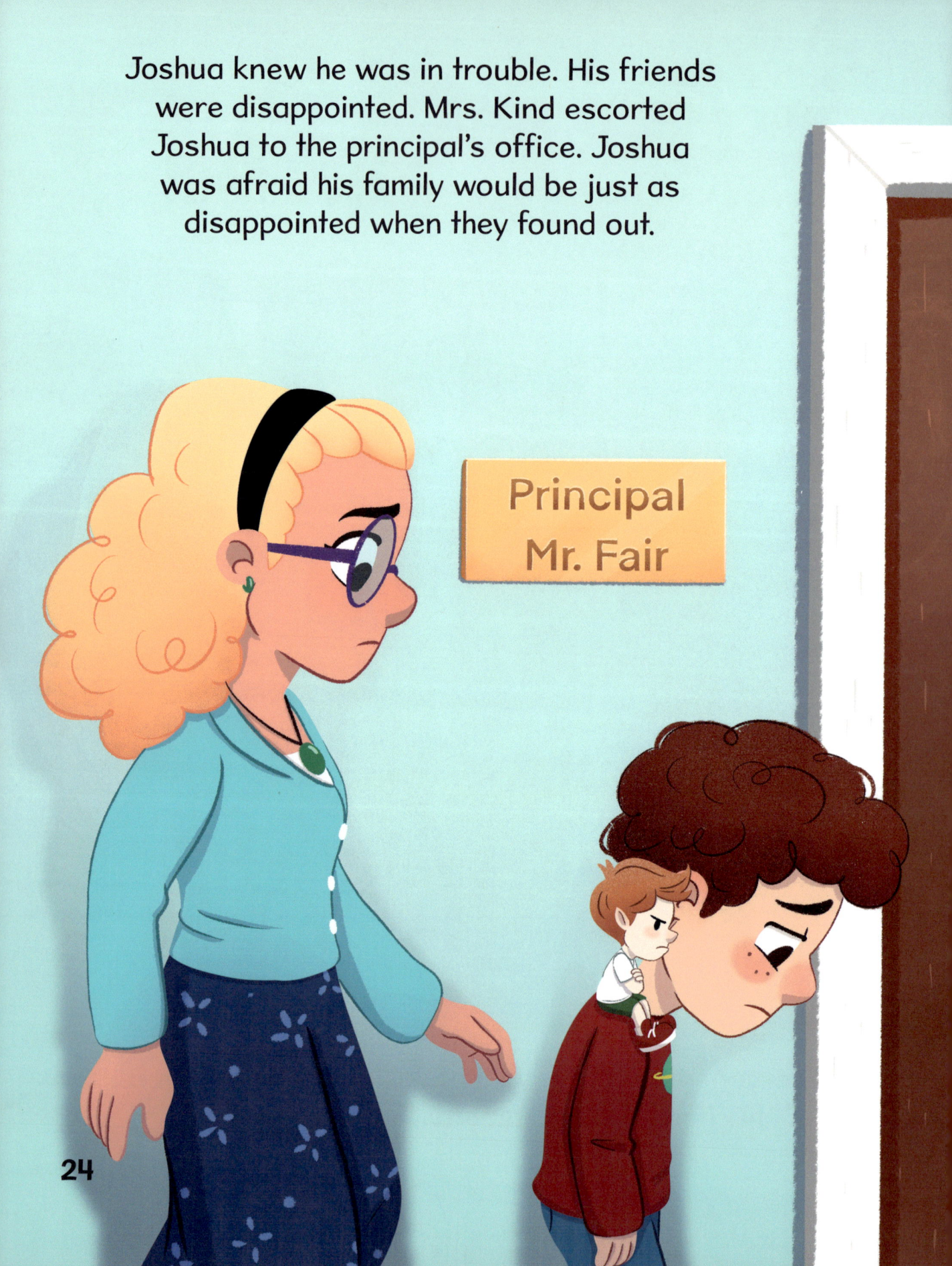

Mr. Fair was not in his office and the waiting was excruciating. Joshua couldn't stand the silence any longer. "Not Me, I don't know why you chose me. I can't take it anymore. Every time I do something wrong, YOU yell out 'Not Me'. Now everyone is fed up with me."

But it's fun to yell 'Not Me'. You don't want to get in trouble, do you?

The principal walked in. "Who are you talking to, Joshua?"

"Nobody," Joshua mumbled. Then he slumped in his seat and sighed. "It was me."

Mr. Fair frowned. "You were talking to yourself?"

"No. Yes. No. I mean … It was me. I accidentally hit Mr. Fast and I accidentally left Hermie's cage open, and I accidentally hit Señora Fork with peas, and I accidentally knocked over the garbage can. And I yelled 'Not Me' each time."

"Thank you for admitting your mistakes, Joshua," said Mr. Fair. "I want the students at B.A. Friend Elementary to ALWAYS take responsibility for their actions. Now, go back to class and help look for Hermie."

Joshua gave the principal a fist bump and left his office.

"Because you're not real, and I want you to go away. You're not any fun!"

Not Me jumped off Joshua's shoulder and, stomping his teeny-tiny feet, he marched out of B.A. Friend Elementary School.

Joshua laughed. "He wants you to read us a story, Mrs. Kind." He picked up a book. "How about this one?"

Mrs. Kind smiled. "You've made a good choice, Joshua."

Joshua smiled. "I sure did," he agreed.

Made in the USA
Columbia, SC
29 November 2024